Fate, Heredity, And Reincarnation

Anna Bonus Kingsford

Kessinger Publishing's Rare Reprints

Thousands of Scarce and Hard-to-Find Books on These and other Subjects!

- Americana
- Ancient Mysteries
- Animals
- Anthropology
- Architecture
- Arts
- Astrology
- Bibliographies
- Biographies & Memoirs
- Body, Mind & Spirit
- Business & Investing
- Children & Young Adult
- Collectibles
- Comparative Religions
- Crafts & Hobbies
- Earth Sciences
- Education
- Ephemera
- Fiction
- Folklore
- Geography
- Health & Diet
- History
- Hobbies & Leisure
- Humor
- Illustrated Books
- Language & Culture
- Law
- Life Sciences
- Literature
- Medicine & Pharmacy
- Metaphysical
- Music
- Mystery & Crime
- Mythology
- Natural History
- Outdoor & Nature
- Philosophy
- Poetry
- Political Science
- Science
- Psychiatry & Psychology
- Reference
- Religion & Spiritualism
- Rhetoric
- Sacred Books
- Science Fiction
- Science & Technology
- Self-Help
- Social Sciences
- Symbolism
- Theatre & Drama
- Theology
- Travel & Explorations
- War & Military
- Women
- Yoga
- *Plus Much More!*

We kindly invite you to view our catalog list at:
http://www.kessinger.net

THIS ARTICLE WAS EXTRACTED FROM THE BOOK:

Credo of Christendom and other Addresses and Essays on Esoteric Christianity

BY THIS AUTHOR:

Anna Bonus Kingsford

ISBN 1564594467

READ MORE ABOUT THE BOOK AT OUR WEB SITE:

http://www.kessinger.net

OR ORDER THE COMPLETE
BOOK FROM YOUR FAVORITE STORE

ISBN 1564594467

Because this article has been extracted from a parent book, it may have non-pertinent text at the beginning or end of it.

FATE, HEREDITY, AND RE-INCARNATION[1]

THE Ego of the regenerate man must dwell entirely in the seventh (or spiritual) sphere, and, as the mystics of the school of St Dionysius say, become wholly absorbed and merged in the Divine Abyss. The selfhood of the man must be lost in the selfhood of God, and become one with It. Not until this final act of saintship is accomplished is the man free of Fate and astral domination, an ascended man, having passed up "beyond all heavens" or starry planes and powers, and "taken captive their captivity." For, indeed, these powers hold us in thrall until they themselves can be bound by us. The ascended man is the type of the elect who have so perfectly taken up their lower nature into the divine, that Matter and Fate, or Karma, as the Oriental theosophists term it, are wholly overcome, and can no more have dominion over them. There is left in them no dross of the sensual and physical planes to weight them down again into material conditions; they are "born again" into the heavenly estate, and have severed the umbilical cord which once bound them to their mother, the earthy estate. Do men become thus regenerate and redeemed in the course of a single planetary existence? Assuredly not. Astrology, chiromancy, phrenology, and other occult sciences, all inform us that every man is born with a certain definite and determinate Fate, which declares itself in his horoscope, on the palm of his hand, in the formation of his head, in the set of his face, features, limbs, and aspect. Speaking broadly, all these determinations are included and intended under the physiological term Heredity, and they belong to the accidents of evolution. But what *is* heredity, and how can it be explained in the light of Eternal Justice? The Macrocosm could not stand a moment were it not founded on a perfect equity and governed by an unalterable law of compensation and of the conservation of energy. Every effect is equal to its cause, and one term presupposes the other. And as the Macrocosm is but the prototype in large of the Microcosm, this also is founded on and

[1] From Anna Kingsford's "Prefatory Essay" to her edition of *Astrology Theologised*, pp. 21-26, 42.—S. H. H.

governed by laws in harmony with those which control the solar system whose offspring it is. So that heredity is no arbitrary or capricious effect appearing without adequate cause, but is the result and expression of foregone impetus, developing affinities and sympathies which infallibly compel the entity on which they act into a certain determinate course and direction so long as the energy of that impetus lasts. Expressed in terms of common physics, this is the law of gravitation and of polarisation. But without this explanation all appears as haphazard and confusion. No hermetist denies the doctrine of heredity as held and expounded by ordinary scientific materialists. But he recognises the sense intended by its inventors as comprising only the last term in a complex series of compelling causes and effects. The immediate cause of a low and afflicted birth is obviously the condition, physical and mental, of the parents responsible, on this plane, for the birth. But beyond this preliminary stage in the enquiry the ordinary scientific materialist does not go. He is unacquainted with the hermetic theorem that all physical effects and results are *ultimates*, which must, of necessity, have their first term in a formative sphere. The corporeal world is incapable of engendering causes, it can but transmit them; hence the beginning of things can never be discovered within the limits of material agencies. Therefore, regarding heredity as the ultimation in physical conditions of causes at work behind and beyond it, the hermetist is irresistibly forced to the conclusion that although a man may be born deaf, dumb, epileptic, idiotic, or otherwise afflicted, because his father or mother have been drunken, immoral, or "unfortunate," these latter causes are immediate only, not mediate, and are themselves in their turn effects of previous causes not belonging to the physical sphere, but to one next above and behind it, that is, to the astral, and that this also in its turn has been influenced by the spiritual energies of the Ego whose "nativity" is involved. And he comes to these conclusions because they are consonant with all that he otherwise knows and has observed of the working of the universe. Many persons find it difficult to reconcile belief in the "ruling of the stars," with belief in free-will. It appears at first sight arbitrary and unjust that certain lines of life—even vicious and base ones—should be indicated by the rulers of nativities as the only lines in which the "native" will prosper; and they ask incredulously whether it can be rationally supposed that the accident of the day and hour of birth is, by Divine wisdom and justice, permitted to control and confine the whole career of an intelligent and responsible being. But the difficulties of astrological science, if viewed in the light of " Karma "—as Predestination—not only disappear, but give place to the unfoldment of a most lucid and admirable system of responsible causation. There is but one hypothesis capable of solving the enigma of Fate, and that hypothesis is common to all the great schools of thought—Vedic, Buddhist, Kabalistic, Hermetic, Platonic—the hypothesis, to wit, of multiple existences. Destiny, in the view of these philosophies, is not arbitrary but acquired. Every man makes his own fate, and nothing is truer than the saying that " Character is Destiny." We must think, then, that it is by their own hands that the lines of some are cast in pleasant places, of some in vicious, and of some in virtuous conditions. For in what manner soever a soul conduct itself in one existence, by that conduct, by that order of thought and habit it builds for itself its destiny in a future existence. And the soul is enchained by these pre-natal influences, and by them irresistibly forced into a new nativity at the time of such conjunction of planets and signs as oblige it into certain courses, or incline it strongly thereunto. And if these courses be evil, and the ruling such as to favour only base propensities, the afflicted soul, even though undoubtedly reaping the just effect of its own demerit, is not left without a remedy. For it may oppose its will [1] to the stellar ruling, and heroically adopt a course contrary to the direction of the natal influences. Thereby it will, indeed, bring itself under a curse and much suffering for such period as those influences have power, but it will, at the same time, change or reverse its planetary affinities and give a new " set " to its predestination, that is, to the current of its " Karma." So that the ruling signs of its next nativity will be propitious to virtuous endeavour. " From

[1] The power of the human will is the instrument by which Destiny may be controlled. In a note to an " Hermetic Fragment," published in *The Virgin of the World*, Anna Kingsford says : " By continued and ardent striving towards the purely spiritual and intelligent, the Soul frees herself from the power of Destiny (Karma), and at length passes into beatitude. She transcends natural order, and enters into the divine. This is Saintship. Inversely, by attaching herself to sensible things, and by suffering herself to be borne away by passion and desire towards illusory existence, she becomes caught on the ever-rolling wheel of Destiny, and made subject to the order of Nature, which is that of Metamorphosis. Whereas her true duty and happiness are to aspire continually upwards, addressing herself by means of purified passion and desire towards the One, and away from the Manifold " (*The Virgin of the World*, p. 150). —S. H. H.

a great heart," says Emerson, " secret magnetisms flow incessantly to draw great events."

The reason why the doctrine of Metempsychosis is not put forward as an article of faith in the Christian dispensation appears to me to be because there is no more death or birth for the man who is united with God in Christ. The Christian religion was addressed to this end, and he who enters the Kingdom of Heaven is saved for ever from that of earth. But very few realise this blessed state, therefore says the Lord, " Few there be that find it." Not, assuredly, that all the majority are lost, but that they return to the necessary conditions again and again until they find it. When once the life of Union is achieved, the wheel of existence ceases to revolve. Now the Church takes it for granted that every Christian desires in this existence to attain to union, such union with Christ being, in fact, the sole subject and object of Christian faith and doctrine. Therefore, of course, she does not preach the Metempsychosis. But, as a matter of fact, very few so-called Christians do attain union; therefore they return until the capacity for union is developed. Such development must be reached in mundane conditions; the cleansing fires of an afterworld are incapable of more than purification; they do not supply the necessary conditions for evolution found only and granted only in this life. Now the dispensation of Christ is the highest there is, because regeneration begins for the Christian in the interior principle, and works outwardly. In other dispensations it begins outwardly and works towards the interior. Buddha, in whose system the Metempsychosis is most conspicuous, is in the Mind, Christ is in the Soul. . . . The religion of Buddha is of the will of Man, . . . for it is by violence that the Buddhist takes the Kingdom of heaven, that is, by the Intellectual way. But they who follow Christ take it by the way of sight, that is, by the Soul. For the Soul is feminine, and does not fight. . . . But the Human will is sanctified, being saved by Christ—the spiritual or seventh principle—and taken into Paradise. It is the Thief crucified on the Right Hand of the Lord, who is taken by Him into Paradise, though not into Heaven. The Thief on the Left Hand is the Creaturely will [—the will of the flesh, inherent in the Creaturely nature—] which must be left behind because it reviles the Lord, even though partaking His Passion. But the Thief who is released unto the mob is the robber Barabbas [—representing the mere Organic or Titanic principle—], who cannot be partaker in the death of the Lord. For the Titanic hath nothing in Christ. So that under Buddha we are born again and die again, but under Christ there are no re-births, for Christ saves us out of the world when we are united to God through His merits and sacrifice. . . .

. . . .

It will be understood, in the light of what has already been said concerning Heredity, that, from the point of view I occupy, original sin should not be taken to imply a burden of corruption arbitrarily imputed to new-born babes as the consequence merely of transgression in a remote ancestry, but as that voluntarily acquired and self-imposed "Karma," which every soul accretes in the course of its manifold experiences, and loaded with which it enters upon each nativity. This weight of original sin may be heavy or light; it may grow or decrease with each successive birth, according to the evolution of the soul concerned, and the progress it makes towards release and light. "If," says Mr W. S. Lilly, "a man submits to the law of moral development by choosing to act aright, he will finally be delivered from all evil. But if he rebels, and will not submit to the elevating redeeming influences, he thereby falls under those which degrade, stupefy, and materialise. And as he would cease to be man had he no free-will, and as moral good implies moral choice, it seems inevitable that he should remain the slave of the lower life as long as he will not choose to break away from it" (*Ancient Religion and Modern Thought*). The spirit of this passage is that of the teaching of Yama—or Death—in the *Katha Upanishad*: "They who are ignorant, but fancy themselves wise, go round and round with erring step as blind led by the blind. He who believes that this world is, and not the other, is again and again subject to the sway of Death."

CPSIA information can be obtained
at www.ICGtesting.com
Printed in the USA
386689LV00007B/22